Teacher
for Guided

POMPEII

Teacher's notes by Alison Kelly
Roehampton University
and Suzanne Maile
Sheen Mount School

Contents

Essential information	*3*
Introducing the story	*4*
Walkthrough	*6*
Independent reading and strategy check	*12*
Return to the text	*38*
Further reading	*39*
Guided Reading Record	*40*
About the Usborne Reading Programme	*42*
The Usborne Reading Programme and the National Curriculum	*44*
The Usborne Reading Programme framework	*46*

Essential information

National Curriculum level: 4C

Genre: historical, factual narrative

Word count: 2,802

Interest words and phrases

earthquake	stonemasons	wares
flagons	Mount Vesuvius	aqueduct
Pliny the Elder	mural	papyrus
pumice	forum	excavations
archaeologists	amphitheatres	

Background

This is a powerful retelling of the disastrous eruption of Mount Vesuvius in AD79 that engulfed the Roman city of Pompeii and many of its inhabitants. Drawing on historical evidence found in eyewitness accounts and unearthed by archaeologists, the book provides a skilful reconstruction of the dramatic events leading up to and surrounding the eruption. The lives of some of those caught up in the disaster are brought vividly to life, and the closing account of the nineteenth-century rediscovery of Pompeii provides a poignant conclusion.

Introducing the story

Before you start the reading session or sessions, spend a little time preparing with your group.

In advance, look out for some images or artefacts representing first-century Roman life: cities, homes, clothing, food, transport and so on, and for some pictures of erupting volcanoes.

Also in advance, look through the book for any names or other words the children may find difficult, and note where they appear. Prepare cards to show the children. You could include pronunciation guides:

Capitoline	ca-**pit**-o-line
Terentius Neo	te-**ren**-tius **nay**-o
Puteoli	pu-tay-**oh**-lee
Via delle Terme	**vee**-a del-leh **tair**-meh
Herculaneum	her-cue-**lay**-neum
Pliny	**plinn**-ee
Misenum	mi-**say**-num
Pomponianus	pom-poni-**ah**-nus
Rectina	rec-**tee**-na
Nucerian	noo-**sair**-ian
Actius Anicetus	**ac**-tius anni-**say**-tus*

Read the back cover blurb to the children and find out if they know anything about Pompeii.

You might ask:

- Do you know where Pompeii is? (In the south of Italy, near Naples.) You could look at the map on page 4.
- Who was in power at the time?
  Elicit "the Romans".

*Latin scholars today would say "anni-**kay**-tus", but you might find the conventional pronunciation is easier for the children.

- What was life like?
  Look at the images you have collected. You might discuss: a huge and well-organized empire; the mighty Roman army; some people very rich, with beautiful villas, others living miserable lives as slaves; and the differences in communications, transport, health, religion and so on between Roman times and our own.
- Look at your volcano pictures too: do the children know of any famous volcanoes and volcanic eruptions? You might like to point out that disasters on the scale of Pompeii are mercifully rare.

Go through the word cards you have prepared, sorting into nouns and proper nouns and explaining if necessary. You could find them in the book and rehearse their pronunciation together.

Share learning objectives with your group.
The children are going to learn or practise the following:
- understanding how authors use time connectives;
- using inference and deduction to analyse characters' responses to the catastrophe.

You might say:
- We are going to look at time connectives (words the author uses to move the story on) and make a note of them.
- We are going to use inference and deduction, or see what we can understand indirectly from the text about how people reacted to the disaster.

When you are ready, go on to the Walkthrough (see over the page).

Walkthrough

The walkthrough allows you to "warm" the text for the children by taking them through it without actually reading it.

- You might use it to identify key vocabulary, language patterns and concepts that children could need support with;
- It can be a way to identify key "thinking points" in the story (for example where predictions might be made, characters' thoughts inferred and so on).

Using a copy of the book, look through it with the children. We have suggested pause points and prompts.

Talk through pages 4-17. As you go along, pick out the features of "normal" Roman life that are depicted.

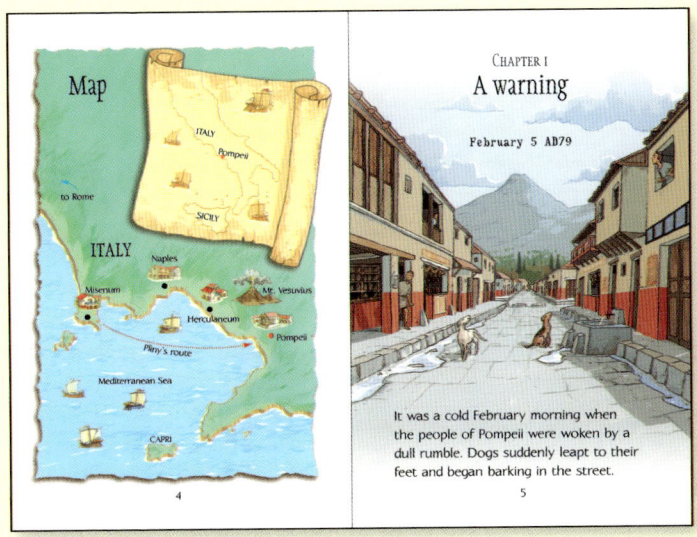

Pages 4-5 set the scene.
- Note the date of the first chapter, making sure the children understand "AD".
- Look at the map on page 4 and the picture on page 5 so that the children have some idea of the distance between Vesuvius and Pompeii.

pages 6-7

Go on to pages 6-7.

- Point out the features of Roman life – the baths and the temple, the passing reference to a slave at work.

Go on to page 11.

- Point out the slaves and market traders.
- Explain the importance of the gods to the Romans.

You might ask:
- What do you think "commerce" means?

pages 12-13

Go on to page 13.

- Point out the time connective, "By ten o'clock".
- You might want to find other time connectives in the book, e.g. "Eventually" (page 25), "As midnight approached" (page 31).

pages 16–17

Go on to page 17.

- Before you start the independent reading, you could introduce the characters of Pliny the Elder and Actius Anicetus, who will feature as the drama unfolds.
- Find the pages where they first appear (Pliny on page 23 and Actius on page 34).
- Explain that Pliny was a wealthy admiral and scholar (he was famous for his writing on natural history). Actius lived far more precariously as a gladiator (make sure the children know what a gladiator is).
- Ask the children to predict how Pliny and Actius might react to the disaster.

The children should now be ready to read independently. This can be done over several sessions, depending on their experience and ability. We have allowed for three sessions, but you might take more or fewer.

Independent reading and strategy check

Before the children begin reading, include a strategy check to help them tackle difficult or unfamiliar words. **You might say:**

- Let's remember what we do when we can't read a word.
  Elicit suggestions from the children, e.g. blend the phonemes, read ahead. You could have your prepared cards to hand to help with difficult Roman names.

Ask the children to read aloud, a little at a time, either all together or in turns, whilst you listen and monitor. Encourage them to use cues to work out unfamiliar words, and praise fluent reading or good use of strategies.

For assessment purposes, you may want to use the chart on pages 40-41 to note strategies that each child uses, or errors or comments that he or she makes, during the reading.

Now ask the children to read chapters 1 and 2 (pages 5-22) whilst you monitor and record strategies.

Remind the children to note down any time connectives as they read.

pages 6-7

And when the local baker, Terentius, returned home, he noticed that his oven had been damaged. The wreckage was everywhere. What had caused it?

An earthquake. But Pompeii was used to regular earth tremors. So no one thought much more about it.

The birds began singing again and people returned to the warmth of their beds. After all, no one had been hurt.

Not yet...

Pause after page 8.
You might ask:

- What impact did this early earthquake have on Pompeii?
  (The children should be able to list the disturbed waters at the baths and the damage to the temple and the baker's oven.)
- What do you think the baker might be saying on page 8?

Now ask the children to read on to page 11.

Chapter II
Vesuvius comes alive

August 24 AD79

The morning started furiously hot – even hotter than a normal August day – but Pompeii's market traders wasted no time setting up their stalls in the Forum. No one spared a glance for the Temple of the Capitoline Triad. Repaired by stonemasons months ago, most people had forgotten it had ever been damaged.

9

Pause after page 11.

- How much time has passed since the first earthquake?
- What is unusual about the day?
- Why do you think there is so much for sale in the market?
  (Think about Pompeii's situation – there is plenty of fresh produce from the country all around, and because it is near the sea, goods are shipped in from all over the Empire, as is confirmed on page 12.)

Now ask the children to read on to page 18.

A shoemaker put out his tools and wine merchants lined up their flagons. Fabric, pottery, wool, bread, honey – thanks to the ships that came to the nearby port of Puteoli, everything was on sale here, as long as the browsers had a few coins in their pockets.

No one noticed that the Sun was looking unusually hazy in the sky. By ten o'clock, the market was in full swing. Traders called out their wares, slaves wandered from stall to stall, buying everything on the day's shopping list.

pages 12-13

In a corner, an old man with a stoop was busily adding his own graffiti to Pompeii's local notice board – a city wall. With no telephones or postal service, this was the way most people in Pompeii left messages for each other.

But this man wasn't happy with what he saw on the wall and he decided to say so:

Oh, wall! I can't believe you haven't fallen down under the weight of all these boring messages!

He rubbed his hands in satisfaction and turned away. But then his chisel slipped and fell with a clatter to the ground.

His eyes were fixed on the horizon as he raised a limp finger to point at what he saw. A blind beggar brushed past him, looking for a few spare coins, and walked into his outstretched arm.

"Give me half a chance, mate. What are you doing, sticking your arm out like that? Could cause an injury!"

But the old man didn't reply. So the beggar moved on, frustrated, still rattling his alms plate.

Finally, the man seemed to come to his senses, shouting frantically to the people around him. Passers-by looked around over their shoulders – until they realized what he was pointing at.

15

pages 16-17

Pause again after page 18.

- Why do you think most people are not as worried as the old man? (Remember that they are used to "regular earth tremors" and "the occasional flurry of activity from Vesuvius.")

Now ask the children to read on to page 22.

In his haste to get away, the man stumbled into one of the open aqueducts and kicked his way up the stream of water. As he ran, a large flake of ash fell onto his tunic, as softly as a flake of snow.
He brushed it away, leaving a dark smear across the pale linen.

page 19

When he reached his home in the Via delle Terme, he found his wife sitting next to the fountain in their walled garden.
He pulled her roughly to her feet and shouted at her to prepare to leave.

"But where are we going?" she asked.
"Away from that!" he shouted back, his finger pointing at Mount Vesuvius in the background. Without a word, his wife hurried indoors.

Pause again after page 22.

- Can you work out roughly what time of day it is by now? (Probably around noon.)

Suggested session 2

You might like to go over the story so far. What do the children remember from the previous session? Look through the first part of the book to refresh their memories.

When you are ready, ask the children to read chapters 3 and 4 (pages 23-45), whilst you monitor and record strategies.

Remind the children to keep spotting the time connectives (e.g. "with each passing hour", "eventually").

With each passing hour, the plume of smoke streaming out of the volcano had become larger and more ominous.

This hadn't prevented him from keeping to his usual routine: a cold bath followed by a light lunch of bread, figs, and olives, sitting beneath the mural of Venus of the Shell on the dining room wall. Even his nephew, Pliny the Younger, seemed happy to continue calmly with his studies.

Eventually, a slave came into the room to clear away the lunch things. Without turning from the window, Pliny gave him an order: "Get a ship ready for me. Right away, please."

He continued gazing at the smoke that was now hanging over the town like a cloud.

"Out into the bay. I want to get a closer look."

The slave hesitated, wondering if he was brave enough to question his master.

"Are you sure?" he asked. Pliny turned from the window. With the light behind him, it was impossible for the slave to make out the expression on his master's face. He could not see the animated glint in the old man's eye that indicated neither fear nor dread. Pliny only felt excitement.

"Of course I'm sure."

Pause after page 25.

Make sure the children understand what is meant by Pliny's "animated glint".

- Why do you think Pliny is excited?

Now ask the children to read on to the end of the chapter.

Pliny emerged from the house, followed by a small group. Suddenly his sister ran out of the house and broke through the crowd to bar his way.

"Don't try to stop me," he said gently.

"No, no. This came for you," she panted, thrusting a rolled up papyrus message into his hand. Looking at his sister suspiciously, Pliny the Elder unfurled the papyrus and carefully read its contents:

> Help! Send a boat for me!
> Can you see it? Vesuvius is exploding and pumice stones are raining down on us.
> I need to get away!
> Your friend Rectina.

"A change of plan," muttered Pliny, still studying the note. His sister let out a sigh of relief.

"Thank goodness you've come to your senses. I was so worried about you."

But he ignored his sister and looked up at the captain who had been waiting patiently for his orders.

> Carry me to Rectina's house.

"Fortune befriends the brave; we'll set sail right away."

Only Pliny could see the nervous twitch that had started up in the captain's eye.

"Where are we going?" asked the captain.

"To Pompeii, of course!"

No one dared suggest Pliny abandon his plan. No one wanted to look like a coward. It was time for action.

27

Led by Pliny the Elder, a group of men walked purposefully towards the jetty where the ships were waiting to take them right into the shadow of Vesuvius. As they climbed aboard, trying not to look down at the water below them, only a few of the men noticed the unusually choppy sea.

Pliny the Younger and his mother stood at the edge of the jetty, holding on to each other and waving as Pliny the Elder set sail towards danger. They did not know that they would never see him again.

page 28

Pause at the end of Chapter 3.

- Why does Pliny change his mind and decide to go straight to Pompeii?
- What do you think he means when he says "Fortune befriends the brave"?
- What does the last line of the chapter reveal? (In fact Pliny did not go as far as Pompeii, but died, most probably of a heart attack, near the scene of the eruption.)

Now ask the children to read on to page 35.

Chapter IV
Panic under Vesuvius

At six o'clock in the evening, Pliny arrived at the house of his old friend Pomponianus. This was a good place to rest before sailing on to help Rectina and any others to escape. As he settled down for a good night's sleep, the foundations of the house shook badly. Outside, pumice stones fell on the heads of anyone who dared step out for a better look.

"Don't panic," Pliny reassured Pomponianus. "If you must go outside, tie a pillow on your head with a napkin."

29

"Are you sure we shouldn't go and get Rectina right away?" asked his friend uncertainly, as he watched the leaping flames of fire light up the night sky at several points on Mount Vesuvius. The day was drawing to a close, but none of the heat had waned.

"I need to rest first," explained Pliny, as he shut his bedroom door.

Pomponianus turned away from the door and bit his lip anxiously, wondering whether or not to risk running out to give the pigs a last feed for the day.

Neither of them knew how much panic was brewing among the 20,000 people who lived in the city, only a few miles away.

As midnight approached, people poured through the gates of Pompeii. The heat was appalling and people wandered around with cuts and bruises on their faces from the falling pumice stones. Ash lay like a soft carpet over everything. It was difficult to do anything without becoming smeared in black soot. Cracks were appearing in the corners of buildings as the ground shook.

pages 30-31

24

At the Herculaneum Gate, a woman stood with her baby in her arms and her two small girls clinging onto the skirts of her toga. Her cries went unanswered.

Help me, someone! Has anyone seen my husband?

The children cried as the woman's eyes desperately searched the hordes of people for her husband. They had become separated in the crowd.

Did she dare wait for him any longer?

Or should she rush on to the Bay of Naples with their children, hoping that someone would find space for four extra passengers on a boat away from the city?

At the Nucerian Gate, a beggar carrying a sack called out desperately for help. His limp meant he would never be able to walk quickly enough to make a decent escape if Vesuvius erupted.

And Vesuvius looked angry.

Won't anyone take pity on me? I can't escape on my own!

Some people didn't have any possibility of escape – it was their duty to stay put. In the gladiators' barracks, 60 gladiators tried to settle down to sleep. But it was difficult in the heat and the noise.

One of them, Actius Anicetus, lay on his back in his bed and held out a hand in front of his face. He watched his fingers tremble and wondered if he'd ever see dawn break. Gladiators shouldn't feel scared. He'd fought in the amphitheatre, hadn't he? But he had to be brave.

page 34

page 35

> His way was blocked by deep drifts of ash. He looked down at his feet, hidden in the soft, warm piles of ash and wondered how so much could have happened in the few hours that he'd been asleep. He didn't know that a burning cloud of ash had been falling on his city all through the night.
>
> The night sky throbbed with the orange glow of fire. But it wasn't the familiar crackle of flames that lit up the midnight scene. There was another source of light and heat – closer to the ground. Racing down the side of Vesuvius, Actius could see the steady flow of molten rocks, moving towards the city with a deadly speed of 35km (20 miles) an hour.
>
> He instinctively gasped in shock and immediately regretted it. Now his throat was burned dry by the raging heat and toxic gases. He clutched his neck and closed his mouth, desperately trying to breathe through his nose.
>
> 36

Pause after page 35.
You might say:

- This chapter is called "Panic under Vesuvius", but not everyone is panicking. Why do you think Pliny stays calm?
- Why does Actius feel he must be brave?
- How long has it been since the first sign of an eruption earlier that day? (About 14 hours.)

Pause after page 36.
You might ask:

- What are the two sources of light and heat?
  (The flame of the eruption itself, and the molten lava flowing down the mountain.)
- Do you know, or can you guess, what "toxic" means?

Now ask the children to read on to page 44.

page 37

Actius struggled to get enough air – but every breath filled his lungs with poison. Feeling dread and panic in the pit of his stomach, he knew that any bravery he once had had finally deserted him.

All around him rang out the sounds of panic. As Actius began to run through the streets of Pompeii, there were too many disturbing scenes to take in.

pages 38-39

A child lay in the street, as if asleep. Actius rushed past. He could see the deadly blow to the young boy's head and the large molten rock that lay next to him. The edges of the boy's tunic were scorched from the large flakes of ash that had been falling on him.

Close by, a dog chained to a building pulled on his chain in a frenzy – unable to escape but aware of the heat and danger. All around, cries of desperation rang in Actius' ears. There was nothing he could do.

A couple emerged from a building. Actius recognized them as Terentius Neo, the baker, and his wife. In her arms she still grasped the writing tablets she used to keep their accounts. They held their hands out to Actius, begging him to help them carry their belongings out of their villa.

But the gladiator had no time to stop.

"Get to the coast," he shouted, as he pushed past, pulling himself free of the grasp of their fingers at his cloak. "It's your only hope."

Then, with a small nod, they joined the rush of people all heading for the same place – the Marine Gate. As they crowded around the bay, a few even fell into the water, as the crowd surged behind them.

"Drop everything and run!"

Slaves, gentlewomen, farmers, traders, scholars, gladiators – everyone was thrown together in the panic to escape. But escape to where? Desperately, people began to throw themselves into the water, hoping it might save them from the heat. But how could they breathe in the thick smoke?

pages 42-43

> Out in the bay, Actius could just make out Pliny the Elder at the helm of a ship. Everyone in Pompeii knew and recognized Pliny, the admiral of the fleet. He had several evacuees aboard ship with him. They were in a state of panic, pointing in the direction of the city and screaming and shouting.
>
>
>
> The ship was slowly turning around, away from Vesuvius. Actius prayed to the gods that Pliny and his crew would escape the devastation. Then Actius looked behind him towards where the people were pointing, at the city of Pompeii – the city that he had loved and been proud of.

Pause after page 44.
You might say:
- The last time we heard of Pliny, he was taking a rest. What do you think he has done since then?
- The evacuees on his boat are screaming. Do you think Pliny would be panicking? (Remember that it was Pliny who made the decision to sail to Pompeii.)

Now ask the children to read on to page 44.

> He saw that the buildings were being submerged in ash and torrents of mud. Soon the river of mud and deadly piles of ash would reach him too.
>
> Actius opened his mouth and took in a deep breath of air. It felt as though his lungs were burning and the pain was almost unbearable. Bracing himself, he took another deep breath, and saw Pompeii turn blurry as his vision began to fail him. Another gulp of air made him sink to his knees. It was with a sigh of relief that he softly collapsed on the ground.
>
> His helmet and dagger were no good to him now. It wasn't how the brave gladiator had imagined death. For the second time that night, he closed his eyes.

Suggested session 3

Go over the story so far. What do the children remember from the previous sessions? Look through the first part of the book to refresh their memories.

When you are ready, ask the children to read Chapter 5 (pages 46-63), whilst you monitor and record strategies.

- Point out that time has moved forward hundreds of years now. Ask them to look out for the connectives that show this.

CHAPTER V
1860: a city rediscovered

For centuries after the disaster, Pompeii lay buried and forgotten, hidden under layers of dust, dirt and rubble. Occasionally a farmer digging his field would turn up a small fragment of mosaic or sculpture, or a piece of bronze - but nothing more.

Then, in 1748, whispers began to spread that the ruins of some very ancient houses had been dug up by local workmen. Word soon reached the ears of the King and Queen of Naples. Intrigued, they ordered excavations to begin.

Over the next hundred years, all sorts of treasures were discovered and entire buildings began to rise from the ashes. Pompeii became famous as a popular tourist hotspot. Everyone flocked to see the site - not just scholars and archaeologists, but rich young Europeans touring Italy to put the finishing touches to their education.

The excavations were often chaotic and slow. Some excavators made detailed drawings and studies of what they found. But others just grabbed what they could for their private collections. But all that was soon to change...

One morning in 1860, the voice of a workman rang out excitedly. He'd spent hours on his knees, sifting carefully through layers of debris, under the instruction of the inspiring new Director of Excavations, Giuseppe Fiorelli.

Director! Over here!

Giuseppe Fiorelli was young, dedicated and ambitious. The Italian king, Victor-Emmanuel II, knew he had found the right man for the job. For too long, this forgotten city had been plundered by amateurs wanting to take away their very own piece of history. It was time to show Pompeii the respect it deserved.

48

Pause after page 48.
You might say:
- What do you think the Italian king means when he says it is time to "show Pompeii the respect it deserves"? (Think about the respect due to the people who died there, as well as its importance as a historical site.)

Now ask the children to read on to page 53.

With over 500 workmen at his disposal, Fiorelli was determined to do just that.

He walked over for a closer look, pushing his panama hat further back on his head. They peered at a small hole in the earth that indicated another cavity containing ... who knew what? Fiorelli nodded and clapped his hand on the workman's shoulder.

See! There's definitely something here.

Well done, Luigi. Mix up some plaster right away. You know what to do.

page 49

Fiorelli walked towards the top of a small hillock to assess the day's work and to admire the slowly emerging city. He leaned against an olive tree and watched as a line of men with wicker baskets on their backs carried rubble away from the site. Others stood on wooden scaffolding as they removed the debris that had submerged the houses of Pompeii. They worked from the roof down, so as not to disturb any relics.

On one of the far houses, a wall painting had been slowly appearing over the past few days, and Fiorelli felt a flush of excitement.

pages 50-51

Meanwhile, Luigi poured his freshly mixed plaster into the small opening in the earth, sitting back on his haunches as the last of the plaster dripped from the bucket into the cavity.

It would take some time to set. So he stood up and stretched his aching limbs. He might only have been a humble workman, but Luigi was almost as excited as Fiorelli. After all, he'd seen what had already been discovered using this brand new technique.

He didn't like to say it out loud, but Luigi thought Fiorelli was a genius. As the excavation had continued, everyone commented on the cavities that kept emerging and then collapsing as the workmen sifted through the ash from that long-ago eruption. It soon became clear that these holes contained the shapes of

52

page 53

long-disintegrated bodies, captured by the volcanic ash.

Fiorelli was determined to recapture them. So he'd invented a technique of pouring plaster into the cavity through a small hole. When the plaster set inside the cavity, it could be dug out.

In this way they had already recovered the contorted body of a dog, a girl covering her face with a tunic, and a man trying to climb out of a window. The detail was incredible – down to the pattern of a fabric or individual hairs on a person's head. They were a part of history that had been frozen forever.

Which new character would emerge this time?

This is the plaster cast of a chained-up dog in his death throes, found at Pompeii. You can still see the thick collar around his neck.

Pause after page 53.

- **What is the exciting technique that Luigi tries out? Can you see why it is so useful?**
(It means that the archaeologists can preserve information about people and animals, and then keep digging to make more discoveries.)

Now ask the children to read page 54.

page 54

Luigi slung his bucket over his shoulder and walked towards the tent where a simple lunch was waiting.

The next day, Fiorelli and Luigi met at the same spot and peered at the ground.

"It's set, I'm sure," said Luigi.

"Let's start, then," agreed Fiorelli. The two of them knelt on the ground and started to clear away the ash and earth around their new plaster cast. It was slow and dirty work, but they knew it would be worth it. By mid-morning, the details of this new personality were emerging.

"It's a gladiator. We've not had many of them," said Fiorelli.

Pause after page 54.

Ask the children to look back in the book and find Actius running (on page 40). Notice the dog to the left of the picture, and compare it with the cast on page 53.

Now ask the children to read on to page 57.

33

"Look. You can tell from the dagger he's holding. Only men trained in the Capuan schools were allowed to use them."

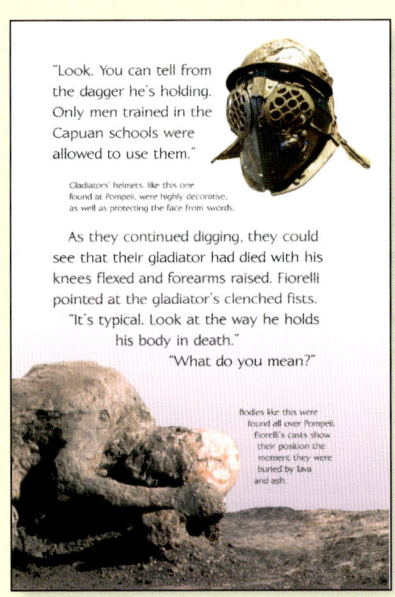

Gladiators' helmets, like this one found at Pompeii, were highly decorative, as well as protecting the face from swords.

As they continued digging, they could see that their gladiator had died with his knees flexed and forearms raised. Fiorelli pointed at the gladiator's clenched fists.

"It's typical. Look at the way he holds his body in death."

"What do you mean?"

Bodies like this were found all over Pompeii. Fiorelli's casts show their position the moment they were buried by lava and ash.

page 55

"It's the muscles. They contract in extremely high temperatures. Any body retrieved from a burning building, even today, will look the same."

"Do you think he suffered?" asked Luigi. Fiorelli tipped his head to one side as he looked at the body.

"He probably suffocated. So he would have been unconscious by the time the ash and molten rocks got to him."

"Still, it's a grim death," murmured Luigi as the two of them stood up again.

"But what a place in history! Immortality! I'm sure a gladiator would have liked that."

The two men bowed their heads as they surveyed the shape of a man who had walked the streets of Pompeii so many hundreds of years before them. This was a gladiator who had slept in a barracks, fought at the Games of Apollo, and bathed in the Temple baths.

"To be a citizen of Pompeii," said Fiorelli quietly. "That was something to be really proud of."

The two men walked away in the fading light. The sea lapped gently in the bay and the leaves of the trees rustled gently in the breeze. All was calm as the workmen downed their tools and set off for home.

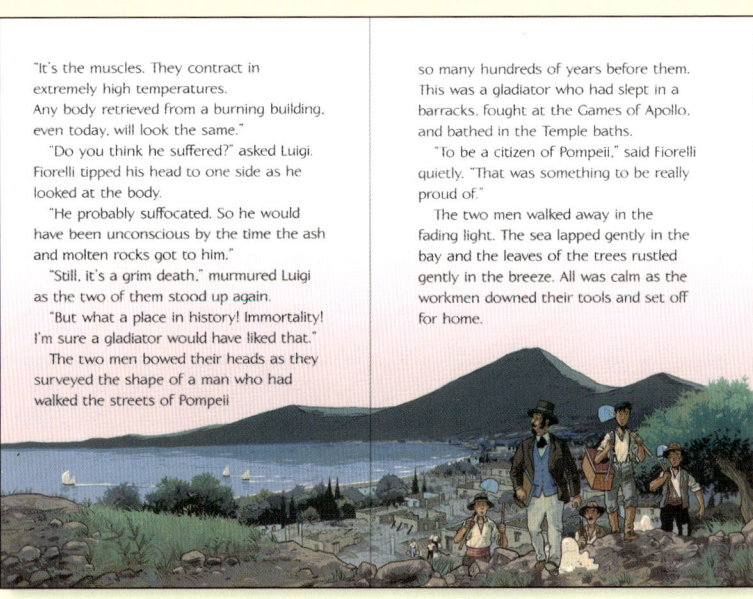

pages 56-57

Pause after page 57.

Check the children's understanding of "immortality".

You might ask:
- Why would a gladiator have liked this?
  Think about the gladiators' fights in front of huge crowds, and how successful gladiators became popular heroes, a little like today's footballers.
- What words would you choose to describe the mood of Luigi and Fiorelli as they made their way home that night?

Now ask the children to read on to the end of the book.

pages 58-59

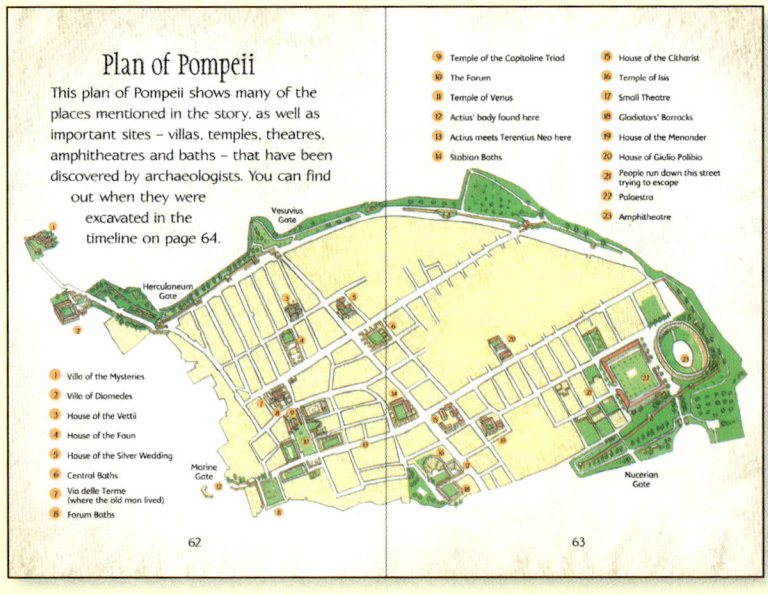

Pause after page 63. (You could suggest that the children look at the timeline on page 64 later, if they like.)
You might ask:
- What do the treasures on pages 60-61 tell us about the people of Pompeii?
- Do the treasures make them seem more real?
- Which one do you like best?

Now return to the text (see over the page) to discuss whether the children's answers and predictions were correct, and talk about their approaches.

Return to the text

The return to the text allows you to reinforce teaching points, e.g. checking children's understanding, identifying and reinforcing successful decoding strategies.

Look through the story again to recap on strategies the children have used for decoding unfamiliar words (e.g. phonic, graphic, context or syntax).

You might say:
- I really liked the way (*child's name*) worked out how to read (*word or phrase*) – can you tell us how you did it?

Talk about the story as a whole.

You might ask:
- Were there any parts of the story that surprised you?
- Which part (or character or picture) did you like best?
- Do you know any other stories like this?
  You may find the children suggest other accounts of Pompeii and the eruption, other stories of Roman times *or* accounts of other natural disasters – help them to think of all the possibilities.

Further reading

Pompeii is in **Series Three** of the **Usborne Young Reading** series. These are some of the other titles in Series Three.

 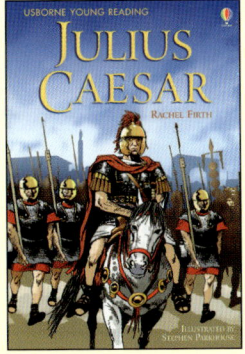 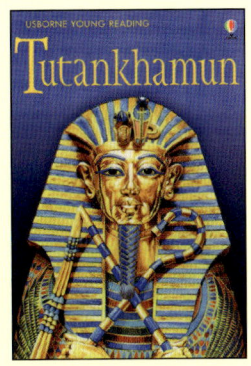

 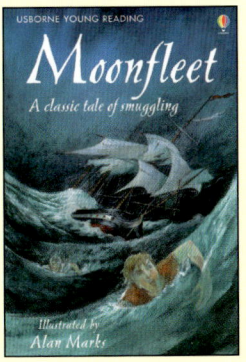 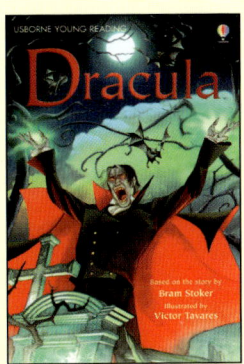

There are over 100 titles available in the Young Reading series, and more are being added all the time. To find out about all the titles available, go to **www.usborne.com**

Guided Reading Record

Text: *Pompeii – National Curriculum Level 4C*

Class: ....

Group: ....

Date: ....

Teacher/
Teaching Assistant: ....

At Level 4C, it is expected that children:

1. Respond to a range of texts including details of character.

2. Are introduced to skimming and scanning.

3. Begin to recognize inference and deduction.

4. Begin to compare texts of significant children's authors.

5. Can use a dictionary, a thesaurus, an encyclopedia and ICT.

These pages may be photocopied for class records, or further copies may be downloaded from **www.usbornebooksforschools.co.uk/guidedreading**

Name:	Name:
Comments:	Comments:
Target:	Target:
Name:	Name:
Comments:	Comments:
Target:	Target:
Name:	Name:
Comments:	Comments:
Target:	Target:

About the Usborne Reading Programme

The Usborne Reading Programme is a collection of over 150 titles for beginner readers, graded in seven levels from very beginners to fully confident readers. Launched in 2002, it has since sold almost 5 million copies worldwide.

The Usborne Reading Programme combines vivid, engaging writing with captivating full-colour illustration on every page. From classic tales to lively non-fiction, there is something to appeal to everyone.

From one level to the next, there is a clear progression in terms of subject, style, narrative length, sentence structure and vocabulary, giving children the satisfaction of mastering real books and making measurable progress without overstretching them and causing them to lose enthusiasm.

Non-fiction titles at all levels draw on the expertise of a range of specialists in their subject, ensuring that the books are not only engaging but authoritative: for example, Eva Schloss, stepsister of Anne Frank, advised on **Anne Frank**, and John Woolley of the Captain Cook Memorial Museum in Whitby advised on **Captain Cook**.

The Reading Programme advisers

The Reading Programme has been developed in consultation with **Alison Kelly**, a leading expert in the teaching of reading, who helped to draw up the seven-level framework (see pages 46-47). Alison worked for many years as a primary school teacher in London, and is currently a Senior Lecturer in Education at Roehampton University, teaching about all aspects of literacy.

Suzanne Maile is assistant headteacher at Sheen Mount Primary School in south-west London, a thriving school with a reputation for outstanding teaching and learning. Suzanne is responsible for curriculum development and initial teacher training at Sheen Mount, and has extensive experience in teaching guided reading at all levels. She is also a teacher tutor at Roehampton University, and a consultant teacher for Richmond LEA.

Together, Suzanne and Alison have chosen a selection of titles from the Reading Programme that are particularly suitable for guided reading, and produced comprehensive teacher's notes, packed with ideas and guidance for guided reading sessions.

The range of titles in the Reading Programme provides wide scope for further reading at every level.

The Usborne Reading Programme and the National Curriculum

The Usborne Reading Progamme is fully integrated with the National Curriculum for English at Key Stages 1 and 2, encouraging children to develop fluent and accurate reading across a range of texts, subjects and styles.

Selected titles from all levels of the Reading Programme are available as Guided Reading packs, comprising six copies of the book plus comprehensive teacher's notes. Guided Reading packs represent a selection of text types, and are carefully graded within levels 1-4 of the National Curriculum.

Text type:
European folktale
NC level: 1C

Text type:
Asian folktale
NC level: 1B

Text type: adapted children's classic
NC level: 1A

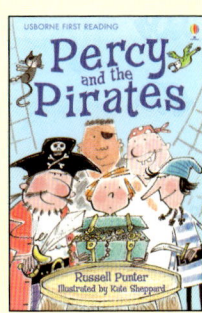

Text type:
original fiction
NC level: 2C

Text type:
original fiction
NC level: 2B

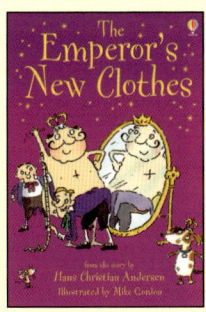

Text type:
classic fairytale
NC level: 2A

Text type:
myths and legends
NC level: 3C

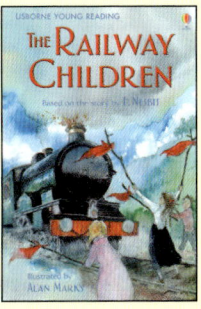

Text type: adapted
children's classic
NC level: 3B

Text type:
adapted classic
NC level: 3A

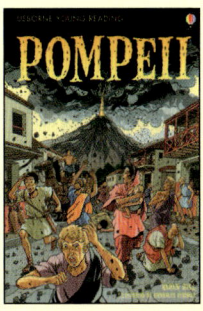

Text type:
non-fiction (history)
NC level: 4C

Text type:
biography
NC level: 4B

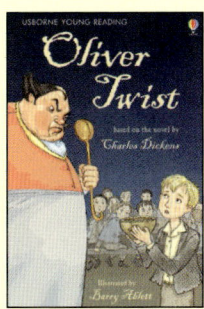

Text type:
adapted classic
NC level: 4A

The Usborne Reading

	Number of words	Themes
First Reading Level One National Curriculum level 1	up to 150	Classic tales (e.g. Aesop's Fables) and folktales
First Reading Level Two National Curriculum level 1	up to 250	As Level One, including less familiar folktales
First Reading Level Three National Curriculum level 1-2	up to 450	As Level Two plus original fiction and non-fiction (natural history life cycles)
First Reading Level Four National Curriculum level 2	up to 750	As Level Three plus classic fairy tales
Young Reading Series One National Curriculum level 2-3	1,000-1,500	Fairy tales, fantasy, fiction, non-fiction ("the story of...")
Young Reading Series Two National Curriculum level 3	2,000-2,500	As Series One plus adapted classics
Young Reading Series Three National Curriculum level 3-4	3,000-5,000	History, biographies classics

The elements above are intended as guidelines only, an whilst distinctions between different levels remain clea

Programme framework

Content	Vocabulary
Short single narrative followed by reading and comprehension puzzles	Simple everyday vocabulary, familiar items
Single narrative plus character sheets and/or maps, and puzzles	More descriptive and evocative vocabulary, always clear in context
Single narrative with repeated elements, plus character sheets and/or maps, no puzzles	Powerful verbs and adjectives, clear in context
Single narrative	More exotic elements and controlled use of idiom
Several linked stories or one longer narrative in chapters. Direct and indirect speech, intertextual references	Wide-ranging everyday vocabulary
Single narrative in chapters. Introduce irony and subplot, allow opportunity for inference and deduction	More challenging, building on Series One; specialist or technical terms explained
Single narrative in chapters. Assumes some relevant background knowledge	Building on Series Two, may assume knowledge of specialist or technical terms

Exceptions may sometimes be made to individual specifications in the interests of narrative or style.

Edited by Mairi Mackinnon
Designed by Katarina Dragoslavic

First published in 2008 by Usborne Publishing Ltd.,
83-85 Saffron Hill, London ECIN 8RT, England. www.usborne.com
Copyright © 2008 Usborne Publishing Ltd.

All rights reserved. No part of this publication may be reproduced,
stored in a retrieval system or transmitted in any form or by any means,
electronic, mechanical, photocopying, recording or otherwise
without the prior permission of the publisher.
The name Usborne and the devices ♀ ☻ are Trade Marks of
Usborne Publishing Ltd. Printed in China.